Ten Shed Fred

Written by
Cath Jones

Illustrated by
Andy Hamilton

One day, Fred said to his mum, "It's a sunny day. Can we go to the shops?"

"Oh no, not again!" said Mum. "Do you need to get extra stuff?"

"Yes," said Fred.

In the shop, Fred got a giant trolley.

He put so much stuff in the trolley!

(Gosh, Fred. Do you need **all** this stuff?)

When he got home, Mum said, "Fred, there is no room in the house for all this stuff. It will have to go in the shed!"

So Fred crammed all the stuff from the shop into the shed!

The next day, Fred went back to the shops!

This time, he put crayons, games and clay into his trolley.

Without delay, Fred took his haul to the shed!

"Oh no," said Mum. "This is just too much stuff!"

Fred went to the shops again and again.

Every time he went, he scouted around for the best offers.

There was so much stuff he could get!

Every time he went, he filled his trolley to the very top.

As the weeks went on, Fred got loads of extra stuff from the shops!

He went to visit the zoo as well — but (oh no!) it had a shop!

He came home from the zoo with a donkey and a snake!

"No way!" said Mum. "I will not have a donkey and a snake in the house."

"But what if they escape?" asked Fred.

So Fred got another shed, just for them!

As time went on, Fred got loads of extra stuff.

He had to get loads of extra sheds to put it all in!

Soon there was very little room left in the garden.

But then, one day, Mum went to the shops to get some stuff too!

She got some new hammers, some timber and some nails!

"Now **you** need a big shed!" said Mum.

But this shed was not for Fred's stuff.

This shed was for Fred. It was his new home!

If only Fred had not got so much stuff.